The

Raccoon

Handbook

Copyright Notice

Disclaimer and Terms of Use

This book is a general educational health-related information product. As an express condition to reading this book, you understand and agree to the following terms. The books content is not a substitute for direct, personal, professional medical care and diagnosis.

The Author and/ or Publisher of this book is not responsible in any manner whatsoever for any consequential damages that result from the use of, or the inability to use this book.

First Printing, 2014

ISBN-13: 978-1500785789

The Raccoon Handbook

Housing - Feeding And Care

Alkeith O Jackson

CONTENTS

Raccoons And Their Relatives

The carnivorous or meat-eating animals have lots of species and families, many of which are far too large, savage, or dangerous to be kept as pets. Nevertheless, many of the carnivores make docile, gentle pets and the common dog and cat both belong to this group.

Many of the carnivorous animals which when fully grown are savage and dangerous are very gentle and playful when young; and even young tigers, lions, and leopards are interesting, playful, and harmless creatures until they are pretty well grown. Such creatures cannot be recommended for pets, but many of the smaller carnivorous animals make splendid and extremely interesting pets.

Some of these animals are very odd and have amusing habits and ways, while others are very intelligent, learn many tricks readily, and are just as desirable companions or pets as dogs, cats, or rabbits. Carnivorous animals are found in nearly every country, and many of them are natives of America. One of the most common and most readily domesticated of American carnivorous animals is the raccoon.

This well-known creature is found throughout the United States wherever there is forest growth and, although continually hunted and trapped, is so intelligent, so wary, and so well able to look out for himself that the species is still fairly numerous in nearly all parts of the country, even near cities or in thickly populated districts. "Coons," when taken fully grown, are, like most wild animals, very cross, irritable, and vicious in confinement, although with kind treatment and patience they may often be thoroughly domesticated.

Young raccoons, when reared in confinement, are as gentle and docile as kittens, and learn to perform many amusing tricks, to come when called, and to follow their master about as readily as a well-broken dog. Raccoons make their homes in hollow trees, in old crows' or hawks' nests, or even among rocks, or at times in burrows in the earth.

If you can locate a coon's nest in winter by following the tracks on the snow, it is comparatively easy to get the young ones in the spring, but otherwise it is a very difficult matter to find the home of one of these animals.

If raccoons are abundant some local hunter or a farmer can usually procure young ones if well paid for them, and oftentimes they may be found in captivity and for sale at the dealers'. Several firms make a specialty of live wild animals and can always furnish many interesting and desirable pets. Coons are almost always carried in stock by these dealers and are far from expensive.

Raccoon Housing And Care

Coons should be kept in large, stout, roomy cages until thoroughly tame and tractable. They are powerful creatures for their size and will work steadily for hours at a time to pry apart loose wires or bars or to enlarge a small opening; hence care should be taken to have a cage that will withstand all their attempts to escape.

Wood will not answer except for young raccoons, for a full-grown coon will chew and bite through a stout wooden bar or board in a very short time. Strong, coarse-meshed wire netting is the best material to use, and it should extend well into the ground if placed out-of-doors.

Although raccoons do not burrow or dig naturally, they can excavate a hole rapidly and will dig under an ordinary fence or wall or beneath the netting of a cage unless it runs at least 18 inches below the surface.

The top of the cage should be roofed over with netting and covered with a water-proof roof and a scraggly tree or stump should be placed within the cage for the animals to climb on. If the cage is to serve as permanent quarters for the coons it should be at least 8 feet square and 6 feet high, but if merely intended as an enclosure for the animals until they are well grown it may be much smaller.

Coons are very restless, curious, busy creatures and are incessantly investigating every crack and crevice or any new or strange object which they see, and this habit makes them very interesting and amusing. A bright-colored wooden ball will sometimes amuse one of these animals for days, and if a piece of corn or a bit of meat is placed in a deep bottle and given to the raccoon you will have no end of fun watching the little chap trying to extract it.

Feeding Raccoons

Raccoons eat almost any sort of animal or vegetable food. They are very fond of green corn and "roasting ears," of many fruits, such as apples, peaches, pears, etc., of young birds or poultry, of eggs, and of any kind of fresh meat.

They are extremely fond of insects of all kinds, of frogs, turtles, fish, and crabs, and will dig under rocks and fallen trees in their search for lands nails.

Tame coons often equal any cat in their ability to capture rats and mice, but they are also sworn enemies of poultry; if you have a tame coon and keep chickens or ducks make sure that your pet cannot reach them or you will regret the day he came into your possession. Raccoons have a habit of soaking their food in water and will even place opened oysters in water before eating them.

So pronounced is this trait, that in Germany they are known as Washing-Bears, and their scientific name of Procyon lotor—meaning a "washer"—was earned by this odd trick. No one seems to know its cause. It is not due to a desire for cleanliness nor to soften the food, for coons have splendid, stout teeth, and such a tender object as an oyster cannot require softening.

Probably it is an instinct which originated with the remote ancestors, who may have subsisted mainly on fish. They are fond of fish and can catch them adroitly. Their method is to sit or squat motionless beside a pool or pond, and when a fish appears to scoop him quickly from the water with a lightning-like sweep of the front foot.

Pretty nearly anything and everything that tame coons will eat is good for them, but raw meat has a tendency to make them cross, and unless they have a great deal of exercise their coats will become poor; and if overfed they will become terribly fat.

A healthy coon should be well rounded and plump but not a helpless ball of fur. Although raccoons are closely related to bears, their appearance and habits are very different. The markings on a raccoon's face give him an odd, quizzical look, and the thumbs and forefeet are used almost like hands.

A coon sitting on his haunches and examining some object held in his hand-like paws seems almost human, and there is no question but that they possess intelligence far above that of most animals.

While our common raccoons are very interesting and attractive pets, some of their cousins are even more desirable. The tropical Crab-Eating Raccoons of South and Central America are somewhat smaller and thinner than our northern species, but are easily tamed and make just as good pets.

The Raccoon-Fox

Somewhat resembling the raccoon but with a form more like a fox, is the raccoon-bear, or raccoon-fox of our Southwestern States. This pretty little animal is smaller than the raccoon, with a much slenderer and more graceful form. Its color is dull, or grayish-brown, with a black streak or collar on the neck and the long, bushy tail is ringed with alternate stripes of black and white.

In Mexico this animal is known as tepe-maxtla, or caca-mixtliy meaning Bushcat or Rushcat, and is a favorite pet of the natives, for it is companionable and gentle and keeps the houses free from rats, mice, and vermin. Although naturally a southern animal, it is found as far north as Oregon and Indiana, and specimens have even been taken in Ohio.

In California it is quite common, and in the early days the gold-miners frequently kept the little creatures in captivity. It is naturally a tree-dwelling animal and makes a moss-lined nest in a hollow tree or other cavity, often using some hole or crevice in the garret of a building or outhouse.

As the raccoon-fox has a peculiar habit of gnawing the wood around its hole, its retreat can often be found by the chips lying on the ground beneath it. Not at all a timid animal, it frequently enters camps, buildings, or houses in search of food.

It is very easily tamed and becomes so sociable and familiar that it seems more like a kitten than a wild animal and will play and frisk about, feed from the hand, and follow its master. Even when captured fully grown, it soon becomes domesticated and docile and is altogether one of the best pets one can find.

In its wild state the caca-mixtli feeds upon small birds, animals, and insects, but when tamed it will eat any kind of animal food and many kinds of vegetables, as well as cake, fruit, eggs, and fish. It breeds readily in confinement and usually has four young in a litter.

The Coati

Another odd and interesting cousin of the raccoon is the coati, or tejon, of Mexico and South America. This animal is about the size of a raccoon, of a reddish-brown above, and yellow or orange below, and with a long, tapered, bushy tail, ornamented with alternate dark and light rings.

The hind quarters are heavy and resemble those of a bear, the front feet are remarkably flexible and hand-like. The most remarkable part of the coati's anatomy is the nose. This organ is greatly elongated and sensitive, and can be bent and twisted, extended, contracted, or made rigid, at will.

There are two species of the coati, one found in Mexico and Central America, the other in South America, but they are very similar in habits and appearance. Unlike the raccoon, these creatures live together in troops or bands, although the old males often become solitary and live by themselves, a fact that has led many people to assume that there are several distinct species.

The coati is very easily tamed and becomes intensely affectionate and devoted to its home and master. It is the most interesting and amusing pet imaginable and keeps one constantly entertained by its antics. Probably no animal in the world is more inquisitive and its incessant investigation of everything in the vicinity continually involves it in difficulties.

In all its actions the coati's nose is a matter of vast importance. With this wonderful organ it explores every nook, crevice, and cranny, smells of any object that arouses curiosity and, regardless of consequences, pokes it into anything and everything. This trait is really a nuisance if the creature is allowed to roam at large, for nothing is beyond its reach; it will climb, jump, or crawl into places that you would think impossible of access.

The coati is a born tease and if kept where there are dogs or cats it will worry them into a perfect frenzy. Moreover, the coati does not know what fear is and, instead of avoiding the anger of its victims, will stand its ground or rush blindly at the enraged cat or dog regardless of consequences.

A coati kept in confinement some years ago was allowed perfect freedom at times and some of its experiences and actions were most amusing. Anything hollow would instantly excite its curiosity: the dinner bell was at once seized and turned over but was altogether too simple an affair for the busy creature to spend time on.

A round sleigh-bell set it wild with excitement, but as it could not get either nose or paws inside and could make no impression with its teeth, it was soon abandoned.

A tobacco-pouch and pipe soon aroused the curiosity of Miss Coati and, holding the first between her paws, she dug her nose into the contents and with wonderful rapidity rooted the tobacco about until every shred and fiber was separated; but finding nothing of further interest here she turned her attention to the pipe. Without the least hesitation she plunged her delicate nose into the bowl, but neither this nor the tobacco seemed to disconcert her in the least.

She soon espied the cat, which, having just finished a nap was yawning and stretching herself. Instantly the coati rose on her hind feet, threw her arms around the cat's neck, and plunged her tobacco-covered nose into the strange cavity presented by tabby's open mouth.

The reception which this intrusion received was a great surprise and, with a most pained and grieved expression, she retreated into a corner of the room and, taking her nose in her paws, drew it between them, sneezing violently meanwhile.

The lesson was soon forgotten, however. In a few moments she was busily engaged in satisfying her curiosity again. Climbing onto her master's lap she noticed the ticking of his watch, and the ever-useful snout was plunged into his vest pocket. Failing to extract the timepiece in this way, she dug excitedly with her feet and, finding this of no avail, placed her ears close to the sound and listened quaintly to the ticking.

At last, quieting down, she dozed off to sleep in her owner's lap and he buried himself in a book. Suddenly, aroused from his reading by the sound of tearing paper, he looked up just in time to discover that the coati had quietly extracted a pocket diary and a five-dollar note from his pocket and was busily engaged in tearing the note into small shreds.

To determine if the coati could drink from a deep, narrow vessel, a mug containing a little milk was given her. Instantly she turned the proboscis up to the forehead and licked the cup dry without even wetting her nose. Quite as easily the nose could be turned down until it actually pointed backward under the lower jaw, and if placed out-of-doors on the lawn or in the garden the creature would rapidly root and plough up the ground with her snout, using it exactly like a hog; and whenever a worm or insect was found the nose would be curved up over the forehead and the object seized and devoured greedily.

Her tail was almost as useful as her nose. If, when tied to a chair or table, an egg was placed on the floor beyond her reach, she would turn her tail toward the object, curve the tip into a hook and, holding the tail with her feet, would gently swing it around in a semicircle with the egg safely held in the curved tip until within reach of her paws.

In a wild state, or in captivity, the coati will eat and drink almost anything. Birds, animals, fruits, insects, fish, eggs, reptiles, vegetables, sweets, grubs, worms, and, in fact, any edible material, is equally relished by it, and in extracting birds' eggs from holes and withdrawing insects from crevices in the bark the prehensile nose is used to great advantage.

Even more interesting is the strange creature known as the kinkajou of South America. This odd animal is also known as the potto, matilla, and fruit bear and is such a mass of contradictions and paradoxes as to be a sort of animal puzzle. Although classed among the carnivore, the teeth of the kinkajou are more like those of an herbivorous creature.

Its hands have no opposed thumbs and the "fingers" are webbed for nearly their whole length; yet it uses these members for hands in a most dexterous manner.

While the heels of the hind feet are well raised, it walks on the soles of the forefeet. It can feed itself equally well with either its front or hind feet and can even hold food in a hind foot and break it in bits and carry the pieces to its mouth with a front foot or vice versa. Its tail is prehensile and, with the tip coiled around a branch, the kinkajou can swing or hang head downward as well as any monkey.

Its face is flat and catlike, but the tongue is so long, flexible, and slender that with it the kinkajou scoops honey from the nests of wild bees or extracts ants from their nests. In fact, the kinkajou may be truthfully said to possess six hands, for its feet, tail, or tongue can be used more skilfully than the hand-like feet of many other animals.

When fully grown the kinkajou is a little larger than a good-sized cat and is light yellowish-brown or orange-yellow in color. The tail is long, round, and muscular, and both body and tail are covered with thick, soft, close, woolly fur.

It is a tree-dwelling animal and spends most of its life high up in forest trees, but can run nimbly on the ground and can descend a tree head first without the least trouble or climb up tail first with equal facility. It is chiefly nocturnal when wild but in captivity seems to be as lively and wide awake in the daytime as at night.

A most wonderful contortionist, it can roll itself into a perfect ball with its tail coiled about its body or can turn itself into a spiral corkscrew without inconvenience. Its food consists of ants, bees, insects, honey, fruit, birds and birds' eggs, small animals, snakes, lizards, etc., and when domesticated it will devour anything in the shape of fruit or meat.

Although quite savage and courageous in its wild state, yet in captivity the kinkajou is most docile, gentle, and affectionate, even when captured fully grown. It is very intelligent and learns many amusing tricks. While living in Central America I had one of these odd creatures for a pet and found it most entertaining and interesting. The little chap was brought in by a native wood-cutter when about half grown and at once won my affection by clambering up onto my shoulders and curling its tail about my neck in a most lovable manner.

It never showed any inclination to scratch, bite, or snap, and from the very first would eat from my hand or climb into my lap and sleep contentedly. It was always happy, bright, and good-natured, and although never tied up or confined it showed no desire to escape, even when perfectly free out-of-doors.

It would sit on its haunches and beg for tidbits with a queer little plaintive squeal but aside from this would never utter a sound. Any new or strange thing would at once attract its attention, but after the unusual object was investigated thoroughly it would excite no further interest. The facility with which it used all or any of its four feet, its tail, and tongue was most remarkable.

Its favorite food was bananas, and if given one of these fruits, it would hold it in one front paw, peel the skin neatly with the other, and eat the fruit with dainty bites and evident relish. If before one fruit was consumed another was handed to the creature, it would hold this in its tail until the first banana was devoured and would then pass it to its paws in a coil of the tail.

Sometimes the fruit would be held in the tail and peeled with one foot and at other times in one hind foot, peeled with a front paw and broken in pieces and carried to the mouth with the other front foot. At other times the little fellow would hang by its tail, curl its head up on its breast, hold a fruit in its hind feet, break it apart, and carry it to its mouth with the front feet. It was very neat and clean, and invariably after eating would pick up all the parings, skins, or crumbs, would gather them in a neat pile, and poke them into some crevice out of sight.

It was so adept with its tail and tongue that it was next to impossible to place things beyond its reach; smooth walls or high shelves it would scale with apparent ease if there was the least roughness or projection which it could grasp with its sharp claws or its tail; and so powerful was the grasp of this latter member that I have seen the kinkajou coil it up, place it flat against a slightly rough board, and actually lift itself off the floor.

Its climbing ability and curiosity proved fatal to our kinkajou in the end. It was placed in a large, roomy outhouse during the night. On a high shelf in this building a jar which contained some preserves had been left through the oversight of a servant.

The following morning the poor little kinkajou was found very sick and the jar of jam was scattered in a thousand pieces on the floor. Evidently the animal had pulled down and broken the jar and had eaten the jam containing pieces of the broken glass. Although we did everything possible to cure it we were unsuccessful. It died the same day.

The Opossum

In many parts of the United States the opossum is a very common animal and is much hunted for its flesh and skin. Opossums make very good pets and have many odd and interesting habits. They are easily captured and tamed, are gentle and docile, but unfortunately sleep during most of the daytime.

Opossums feed mainly upon fruit and insects, but they will eat any kind of meat, eggs, birds, fish, or reptiles. Their ability in climbing and their strong, prehensile tails are interesting, and if a tree or some branches are placed in their cage they will exhibit their ability to climb and swing from place to place to great advantage.

Several species of South American opossums carry their young hanging to the mother's tail as it is carried over the back, but our common species carries its babies in pockets or pouches on the abdomen. Some of the South American species are very small, scarcely larger than a mouse, while others are even larger than the northern species.

One kind of opossum found in South America is known as the Water-Opossum, from the fact that it lives in the water most of the time. This queer animal swims, dives, and catches fish with the ease and ability of an otter or mink and makes its nest in holes in the banks of rivers or lakes.

Although I have included opossums among the carnivorous animals, they are very different from most other meat-eating creatures and belong in a group known as marsupials. This group includes all animals which carry their young in pouches, and among them are creatures which are strictly carnivorous, others which are herbivorous, and others which are insectivorous.

All four-footed animals found in Australia, with the exception of the duckbill, echidna, and the Wild Dog, or dingo, are marsupials. Among them are the kangaroos, koalas or native bears, wombats, bandicoots, ant-eaters, Tasmanian devils, and other queer creatures.

In Australia nearly all of these various animals are at times kept in captivity, and the smaller kangaroos, wombats, and koalas make good pets. Many of the marsupials are nocturnal and are so sleepy in the day that they are not worth keeping as pets except in menageries or zoological gardens, but the kangaroos or wallabies and some other species are wide-awake and lively during the day.

Kangaroos and other herbivorous marsupials are as easily kept as rabbits or hares and feed mainly on hay, grass, and green vegetables and many of them are very hardy and will stand quite cold weather.

The Bear

Among the other carnivorous animals which are kept as pets at times are bears, foxes, and prairie-wolves, or coyotes. Bears when young make very interesting pets and are easily raised. The following story of a boy and his tame bear will illustrate the habits of these animals in captivity.

A FUUNY STORY OF A PET BEAR

Ned always had a fine time when he visited his grandfather, who lived in Maine near the edge of the forest, and when he was twelve years old he spent his summer vacation there. One day Ned noticed that some bees in the garden flew toward the woods instead of to the hives, and when he asked his grandfather the reason he was told that these were wild bees that had a "honey-tree" in the forest.

Ned was greatly interested, and his grandfather promised that they would look for the store of honey, explaining that they could find it by following the bees, which flew in a straight line. Soon after Ned started out with Dave, the hired man, to find the bee-tree.

They found a hollow log among some rocks, and Ned thought this would be a fine place for the bees to hide honey. Dave knew it was not a bee-tree, but to please Ned he chopped into it. After a few good strokes the log split open, and out rolled a big ball of fur. It quickly unrolled and proved to be a baby bear that winked and blinked in a surprised, sleepy manner.

The boys thought this find a great deal better than honey and, wrapping the cub in a coat, they hurried home as fast as they could for fear the old bear might find them. The little bear was given a cozy home in the wood-shed and a big bowl of bread and milk, which he ate greedily.

Then he curled up and went fast asleep. The next day Ned found his pet, which he had named Bee, very contentedly washing his face in the remains of his supper. When he saw Ned he sat up on his haunches and held out his paws in a most friendly and confiding manner. He was full of life and play and rolled over and curled and uncurled himself, and Ned was sure that he could teach him interesting tricks.

Every day Ned played with his pet and by the time his vacation was over the bear had learned to shake hands, to beg for a lump of sugar, to play dead at command, and to turn somersaults.

Ned was very anxious to take Bee back to Boston with him so that his friends could see him; but since his father would not consent to take a bear to the city, Ned was compelled to leave him in his grandfather's charge. Ned's friends were greatly interested in the stories of the bear, and every one of his grandfather's letters was read and reread, for each was filled with glowing accounts of Bee's antics.

One day in November came the startling news that Bee had disappeared. Grandpa had gone to town for the day and had forgotten to fasten the door of the woodshed, and the next morning the bear was missing. The woods were searched and all likely hiding-places were examined, but no trace of Bee could be found. Ned's grandfather felt very badly over the loss and so, of course, did Ned. All winter he and the boys talked about the matter and hoped that the following year he might find another bear.

Early in April Ned had another letter from his grandfather, and when he read it he danced and shouted, for, wonder of wonders. Bee had been found! It seemed that Dave had gone to the sugar-camp, about half a mile from the house, to get the log house ready for the sugar boiling.

He found the camp half full of drifted leaves, and when raking them out behind a big sugar-kettle he discovered Bee, all curled up snug and warm, enjoying his long winter nap. Dave, greatly surprised, tied Bee securely without waking him, covered him with the leaves, and left him.

When sugar making began a few weeks later Bee was wide-awake and hungry, but he knew Dave and followed him readily to his old quarters. When Ned arrived on his vacation he hardly knew his pet; he had grown into such a big, {Powerful bear that he had to be tied out-of-doors in the barnyard; but he was still good-natured and Ned was soon on the best of terms with him again.

Nevertheless, Bee was so big and clumsy and so rough in play that grandpa was afraid Ned would get hurt and suggested that he should sell him to a circus which was coming to a near-by town. At first Ned was unwilling to listen to this, but he realized that Bee was really too big to manage and finally consented.

The animal trainer visited the farm, saw Bee, and was very glad to get such a gentle, well-trained bear. Several times afterward, when the circus visited Boston, Ned saw his old pet.

FOXES AND WOLVES

Unlike bears, foxes and wolves are seldom very docile in captivity. Once in a while a really tame fox or wolf may be found, but as a rule they are snappish, treacherous creatures and can hardly be recommended as pets.

Wolves are far more likely to become really tame than foxes and prairie-wolves or coyotes. They are often very affectionate and tractable in captivity. In order to domesticate any of these creatures they must be taken when very young and reared by hand.

They are not particularly interesting, not half as intelligent as a good dog, and have no particular habits or characters which make it worthwhile keeping them as pets, especially in view of the time and trouble necessary to rear them successfully.

Wolf

Fox

Raccoon

Made in the USA
Monee, IL
23 September 2022

14552742R00022